PURSES
BAGS
& TOTES

moya's workshop

American Quilter's Society
P. O. Box 3290 • Paducah, KY 42002-3290
www.AmericanQuilter.com

Located in Paducah, Kentucky, the American Quilter's Society (AQS) is dedicated to promoting the accomplishments of today's quilters. Through its publications and events, AQS strives to honor today's quiltmakers and their work and to inspire future creativity and innovation in quiltmaking.

EXECUTIVE BOOK EDITOR: ANDI MILAM REYNOLDS
SENIOR EDITOR: LINDA BAXTER LASCO
PATTERN EDITOR: JULIA CHEN
COPY EDITOR: CHRYSTAL ABHALTER
TRANSLATOR: NANA WU
GRAPHIC DESIGN: MELISSA POTTERBAUM
COVER DESIGN: MICHAEL BUCKINGHAM
HOW-TO PHOTOGRAPHY: CHIA-HAN TSAI AND ZONG-YI LIN
ADDITIONAL PHOTOGRAPHY: CHARLES R. LYNCH

American Quilter's Society
P. O. Box 3290 • Paducah, KY 42002-3290
www.AmericanQuilter.com

Additional copies of this book may be ordered from the American Quilter's Society, PO Box 3290, Paducah, KY 42002-3290, or online at www.AmericanQuilter.com.

Text © 2012, Author, Moya's Workshop
Artwork © 2012, American Quilter's Society

LIBRARY OF CONGRESS CATALOGING-IN-PUBLICATION DATA

Purses, bags & totes / by Moya's Workshop.
     p. cm.
   Summary: "Create bags, purses, and totes in no time! Sew any of the 10 projects: Handbags, Messenger bags, Shoulder bags, Backpacks, Eco bags, Tote bags. The book includes easy-to-follow instructions plus full-size patterns on the CD for no fuss construction. Great for gifts, too"-- Provided by publisher.
   ISBN 978-1-60460-029-2
   1. Dress accessories. 2. Sewing. I. Moya's Workshop. II. Title: Purses, bags, and totes.
   TT649.8.P87 2012
   646'.3--dc23
                              2012019347

Table of Contents

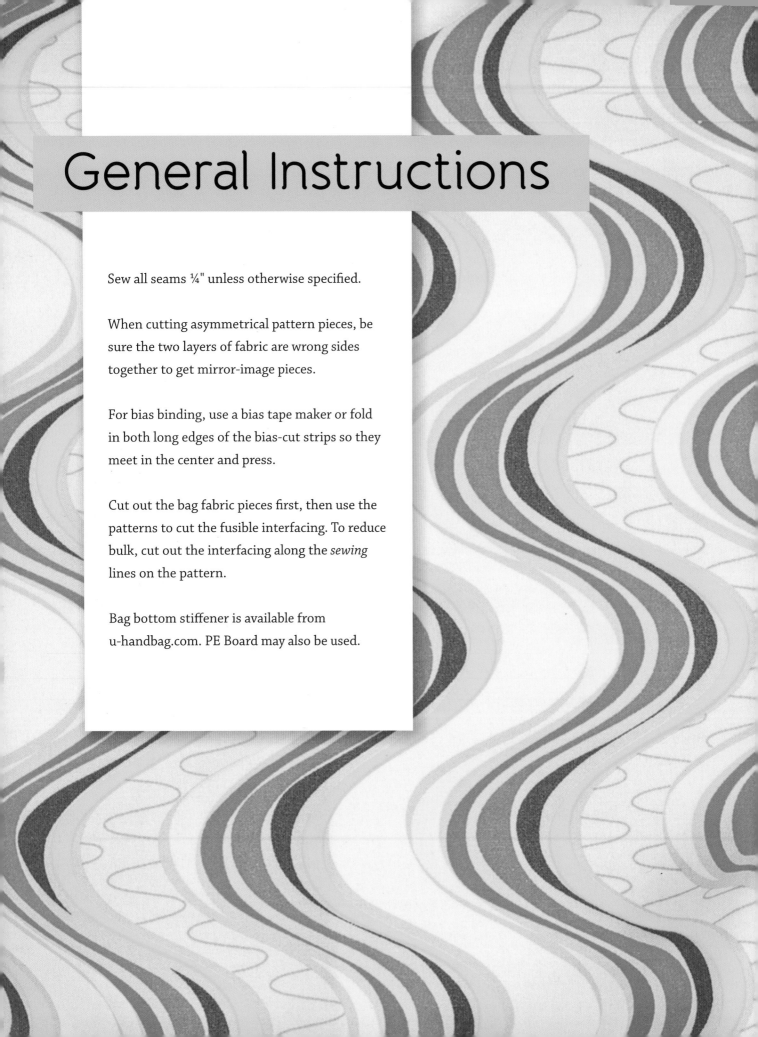

General Instructions

Sew all seams ¼" unless otherwise specified.

When cutting asymmetrical pattern pieces, be sure the two layers of fabric are wrong sides together to get mirror-image pieces.

For bias binding, use a bias tape maker or fold in both long edges of the bias-cut strips so they meet in the center and press.

Cut out the bag fabric pieces first, then use the patterns to cut the fusible interfacing. To reduce bulk, cut out the interfacing along the *sewing* lines on the pattern.

Bag bottom stiffener is available from u-handbag.com. PE Board may also be used.

Pockets

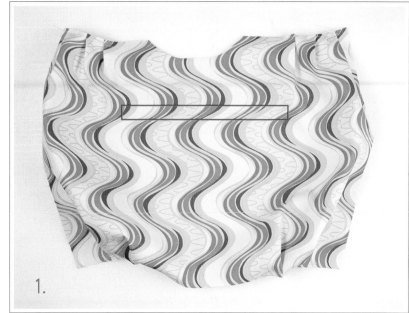

1.

Zipper Pocket

Materials

- One zipper the size specified in the pattern

- Fabric whose dimensions are
  - the length of the zipper + 1½"
  - twice the desired depth of the pocket + 1½"

- Woven fusible lightweight interfacing

- WashAway Wonder Tape

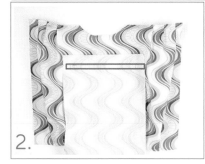

2.

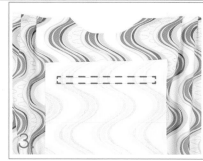

3.

Sewing Instructions

1. Mark a rectangle the same length as the zipper and ½" wide on the main bag fabric where you want the Zipper Pocket opening.

2. Iron interfacing on the wrong side of the pocket fabric and mark the same size rectangle on the interfacing, ¾" from the top. With the pocket and bag fabrics right sides together, align the drawn rectangles and pin in place.

3. Sew around the marked rectangle.

4. Draw a line down the center, stopping ¼" from the ends, then mark from that point to the corners. Cut on the line and to the corners being careful NOT to cut the stitching.

5. Turn the pocket fabric through the hole to the back of the bag fabric.

6. Iron the opening to shape a rectangular hole from the back.

4.

5.

6.

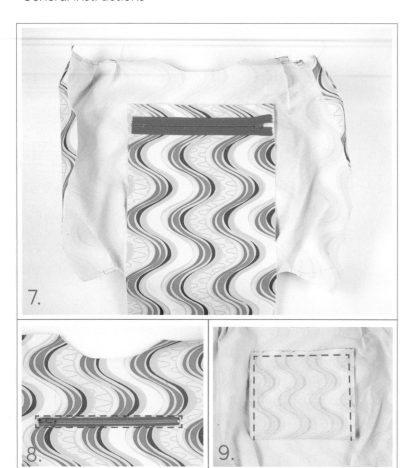

7. Use wash-away tape to position the zipper over the opening.

8. Turn the bag body to the front and sew around the rectangular hole, ⅛" from the edge, to secure the zipper.

9. From the back, fold the pocket fabric in half, right sides together, and sew around 3 sides, being careful NOT to sew the main bag body.

Elasticized Pocket

Materials

- ⅜" wide elastic the length specified in your pattern

- Fabric whose dimensions are 1½ times the desired pocket width and twice the desired pocket depth

- Woven fusible light-weight interfacing the same width as the fabric and the desired pocket depth

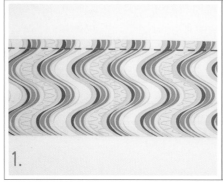
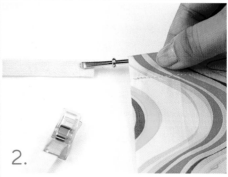

Sewing Instructions

1. Iron the interfacing on the upper half of the wrong side of the pocket fabric. Fold the pocket fabric in half, wrong sides together, and sew a line ½" from the folded edge to create a channel.

2. Use a bodkin to pull the elastic through the channel. Pin or clip the opposite end of the elastic to avoid pulling it into the channel.

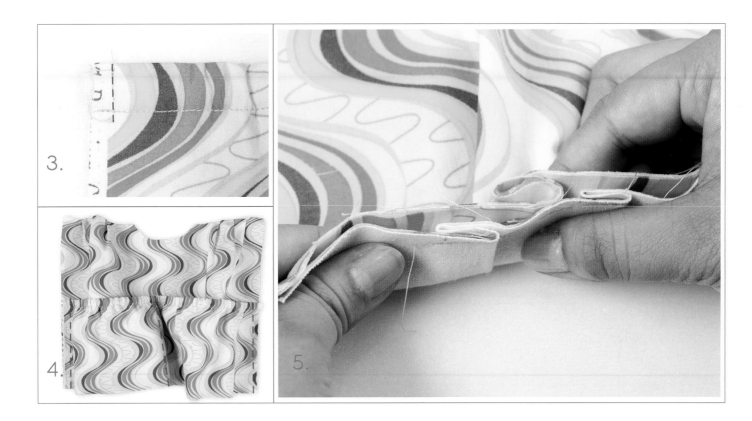

3. Align the ends of the elastic with the 2 ends of the channel and baste them in place.

4. Align the raw edges of the elasticized fabric with the bottom and sides of the Main Body fabric. Stitch a line from the bottom up through the elastic channel to form 2 or more pockets. Then baste the pocket sides with the sides of the Main Body fabric.

5. Make few folds at the bottom of the elasticized fabric until the size matches the bottom of the Main Body fabric. If the Main Body fabric also has several folds, mismatch these folds to avoid too many layers of fabric.

6. Baste the bottom of the elasticized fabric to the bottom of the Main Body fabrics.

Slip Pocket

Materials

- Fabric the desired pocket width and twice the desired pocket depth

- Woven fusible lightweight interfacing the desired pocket width and depth

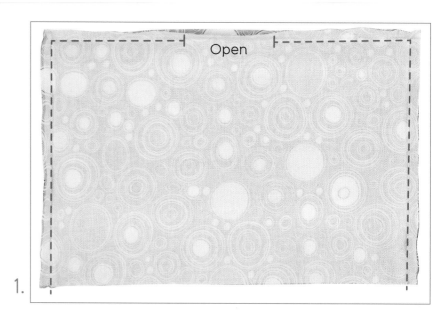

1.

2.

3.

Sewing Instructions

1. Iron the interfacing on the upper half of the wrong side of the fabric. Fold the fabric in half with right sides together and sew as shown, leaving an opening for turning.

2. Turn right-side out through the opening. The folded edge should be the upper edge of the pocket. Topstitch along the folded edge.

3. Fold and iron to form the side pocket. Edge-stitch the folds $1/16$" along the fold.

4. Pin the pocket on the main bag fabric, sew a middle line to form 2 pockets, and then sew around the pocket edge, $1/8$" from the edge to attach the pocket.

4.

Self-Covered Button

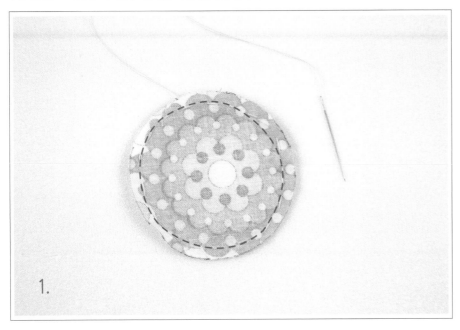

1.

Materials

- One Self-Covered Button
- A circle of fabric whose diameter is twice the size of the Self-Covered Button minus ¼"

Sewing Instructions

1. Sew a basting stitch ³/₁₆" from the edge of the button fabric circle.

2. Put the top of the Self-Covered Button casing onto the wrong side of the fabric. Pull the thread to gather the fabric around the button casing.

3. Press the button washer over the back of the button.

4. By doing so, finish the Self-Covered Button.

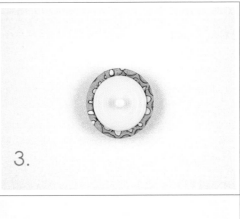

3.

2.

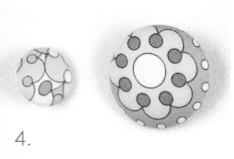

4.

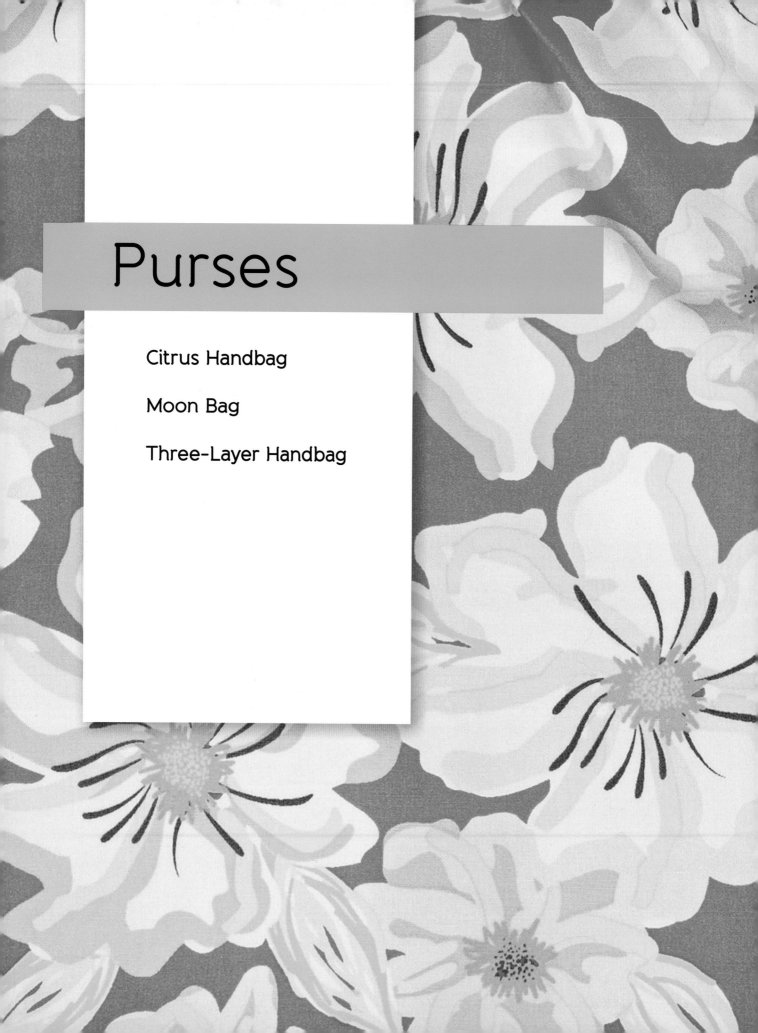

Purses

Citrus Handbag

Materials

- 1 yard woven fusible heavyweight interfacing
- ½ yard woven fusible lightweight interfacing
- One 18" zipper
- One 12" zipper
- Two 8" zippers

- 6 yards ⅛" piping cord
- One pair of ready-made leather handles
- Fabric A (Citrus with white background) – ⅔ yard
- Fabric B (Orange) – ⅔ yard
- Fabric C (Brown) – ½ yard
- Fabric D (Lining) – 1 yard

Cutting and Fusing Instructions

Fabric A (Citrus with white background)

Main Body	2 pieces from the Main Body pattern	Iron with heavyweight interfacing.
Front Pocket	2 pieces from the Front Pocket pattern	Iron with heavyweight interfacing. Choose one piece as the Exterior Front Pocket, and the other as the Lining Front Pocket.
Back Zipper Pocket	1 piece 9½" x 12½"*	Iron with lightweight interfacing.

Fabric B (Orange)

Upper Gusset	4 pieces from the Upper Gusset pattern	Iron with heavyweight interfacing. Choose two pieces as the Exterior Upper Gussets, and the others as Lining Upper Gussets.
Lower Gusset	2 pieces from the Lower Gusset pattern	Iron with heavyweight interfacing. Choose one piece as the Exterior Lower Gusset, and the other as the Lining Lower Gusset.

Fabric B (Orange) continued...

Upper Gusset of Front Pocket	2 pieces 1⅜" x 12½"	Choose one piece to iron with heavyweight interfacing. This piece will be the Exterior Upper Gusset of the Front Pocket fabric.
Lower Gusset of Front Pocket	2 pieces 1⅝" x 15⅜"	Choose one piece to iron with heavyweight interfacing. This piece will be the Exterior Lower Gusset of the Front Pocket fabric.

Fabric C (Brown)

Main Body Piping	2 bias-cut strips 1" x 47¼"
Front Pocket Piping	1 bias-cut strip 1" x 29½"
Upper Gusset Binding	2 bias-cut strips 1½" x 4½"
Lower Gusset Binding	2 bias-cut strips 1½" x 5"

Fabric D (Lining)

Main Body	2 pieces from the Main Body pattern	Iron with heavyweight interfacing.
Slip Pocket	1 piece 11" x 12½" *	Iron with 11" x 6¼" lightweight interfacing.
Zipper Pocket	1 piece 9½" x 12½" *	Iron with lightweight interfacing.
Binding	2 bias-cut strips 1½" x 47¼"	

*Pocket sizes can be adjusted as preferred.

Sewing Instructions

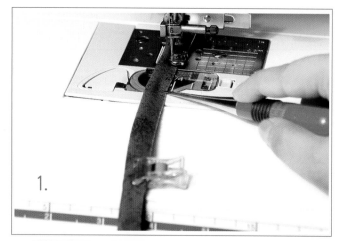

1. Cover the piping cord with the piping fabric using a zipper foot.

2. Lay the raw edges of the piping onto the right side bottom edge of the Exterior Front Pocket. Baste the piping around the Exterior Front Pocket, leaving about 3" at both ends unstitched.

3. Sew the 2 ends of piping cord together with the raw edges overlapping ½" at a 45-degree angle. Trim the rest of the piping.

4.

5.

4. With the raw edges of the piping right sides together, stitch a ¼" seam. Press the seam open and trim.

5. Baste the unstitched piping to the Exterior Front Pocket.

6.

6. Repeat steps 1-5 to make piping for the 2 pieces of the Exterior Main Body fabric. Now the Exterior Main Body with piping and Exterior Front Pocket with piping are finished.

7. Use wash-away tape to align one of the long edges of a 12" zipper with one of the long edges of the Exterior Upper Gusset of the Front Pocket and stitch.

8. Flip right-side out.

9. With the Exterior Lower Gusset of the Front Pocket and the Exterior Upper Gusset of the Front Pocket right sides together, align the short edges and stitch.

10. Press the seam allowance of one of the long edges of the Lining Upper Gusset of the Front Pocket to the wrong side of the fabric.

11. Align the unfolded long edge of the Lining Upper Gusset of the Front Pocket with one of the long edges of the Lining Lower Gusset of the Front Pocket. Stitch the short edges.

7.

8.

9.

10.

11.

12.

12. With the Exterior and Lining Gusset of the Front Pocket right sides together, align the unfolded edge of the Lining Gusset with the long edge without the zipper and stitch.

13.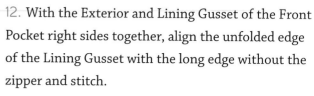

13. Flip right-side out and press the seam toward the Lining Gusset of the Front Pocket. Topstitch ⅛" from the stitched edge.

14.

14. With the wrong sides of the Exterior and Lining Gusset of the Front Pocket together, topstitch the lines around the zipper edges to also stitch the lining together.

15.

15. Baste the raw edge of the Gusset of the Front Pocket.

16.

17.

16. With the Exterior Front Pocket and Exterior Gusset of the Front Pocket right sides together, baste around the Exterior Front Pocket.

17. With the Lining Front Pocket and the Lining Gusset of the Front Pocket right sides together, use clips or pins to hold the fabrics together.

18. Stitch around the Front Pocket, leaving an opening.

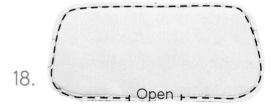

18.

Open

19. Turn right-side out and stitch the opening closed.

19.

Lining

20. Use wash-away tape to make up a three-layered zippy sandwich with the Lining Upper Gusset right-side up on the bottom, the zipper right-side up in the middle, and the Exterior Upper Gusset wrong-side up on top. Match one long edge of the zipper with the Stitching zipper edge of the Upper Gusset.

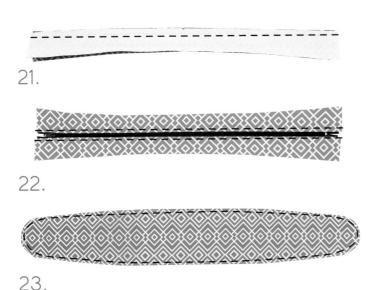

21. Stitch the matched edges. Make a three-layered zippy sandwich at the other long edge of the zipper and stitch as before.

22. Flip right-side out. With the Exterior and Lining Upper Gusset wrong sides together, topstitch ⅛" from the stitched edges.

23. With the Exterior and Lining Lower Gusset wrong sides together, baste around the Lower Gusset.

24. Pass all the binding fabric through the tape maker and iron the folds.

25. With the Upper Gusset Binding and the Lining Upper Gusset right sides together, match and stitch the long edge of the binding with the short edge of the Upper Gusset.

26. Fold the Upper Gusset Binding to the Exterior Upper Gusset and topstitch ⅛" on the binding.

27. With the Lower Gusset Binding right sides together with the Lining Lower Gusset, stitch the curve. Cut a few clips in the binding so it lies flat.

28. Fold the Lower Gusset Binding to the Exterior Lower Gusset and topstitch ⅛" on the binding.

29. Overlap both short ends of the Upper and Lower Gussets according to the pattern and stitch.

30. Make the Exterior Back 8" Zipper Pocket on the Exterior Back Main Body. (Refer to the Zipper Pocket instructions, pages 5-6.)

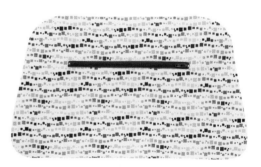

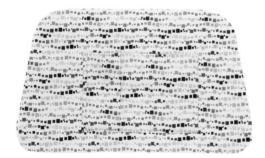

31. Make pockets as desired on the Lining Main Body. (Refer to the Zipper Pocket and Slip Pocket instructions, pages 5-8.)

32. Position and stitch the Front Pocket on the Exterior Front Main Body according to the Main Body pattern.

33. With one of the long edges of the Exterior Gusset and the Exterior Front Main Body right sides together, baste around the Exterior Front Main Body.

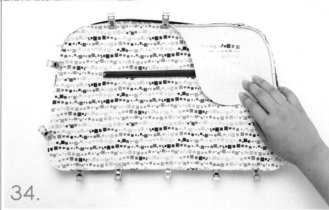

34. Clip or pin the Exterior Front Main Body and one of the Lining Main Body pieces wrong sides together.

35. Stitch the long edges of the Gusset, Exterior Front Main Body, and Lining Main Body together.

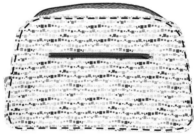

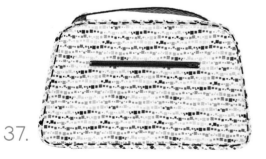

36. Stitch around the Lining Binding and the Lining Gusset, right sides together.

37. Fold the Lining Binding toward the Lining Main Body and topstitch ⅛" along the binding.

38. Repeat steps 33–37 to make the back side of the bag.

39. Turn right-side out and stitch the leather handles to the bag. (See photo, page 11.)

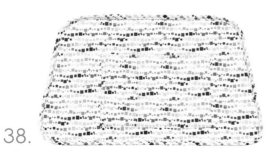

Materials

- 1⅓ yards of woven fusible heavyweight interfacing

- ⅖ yard of woven fusible lightweight interfacing

- 1⅜" x 13" of low-loft polyester batting

- One 5" zipper

- One 7" zipper

- One 14" zipper

- Two 1½" rectangular rings

- Fabric A – ⅞ yard

- Fabric B – ⅞ yard

- Fabric C (Lining) – 1 yard

Moon Bag

Cutting and Fusing Instructions

Fabric A		
Main Body	2 pieces from the Exterior Main Body pattern	Iron with heavyweight interfacing until the stop point (indicated on the pattern).
5" Exterior Back Zipper Pocket	1 piece 9½" x 14"*	Iron with lightweight interfacing.
Fabric B		
Main Body	2 pieces from the Exterior Main Body pattern	Iron with heavyweight interfacing until the stop point (indicated on the pattern).
Fabric C (Lining)		
Upper Main Body	2 pieces from the Lining Upper Main Body pattern	Iron with heavyweight interfacing until the stop point (indicated on pattern).

Fabric C (Lining) continued...

Lower Main Body	2 pieces from the Lining Lower Main Body pattern	Iron with heavyweight interfacing.
Slip Pocket	1 piece 12½" x 12½"*	Iron with 12½" x 6¼" lightweight interfacing.
7" Zipper Pocket	1 piece 8½" x 14"*	Iron with lightweight interfacing.
Shoulder Strap	1 strip 3¾" x 26¾"	Prepare 1½" x 13" of heavyweight interfacing and 1⅜" x 13" of low-loft polyester batting.
Zipper Tab	1 piece of 2" x 2¾"	

*Pocket sizes can be adjusted as preferred.

Sewing Instructions

1. With Exterior Fabrics A and B of the Exterior Main Body right sides together, stitch the center seam to form the Exterior Main Body. Repeat.

2. Press the seam open.

3. Make a 5" Exterior Back Zipper Pocket on one piece of the Exterior Main Body (pages 5-6). Then sew the darts of the Exterior Main Body.

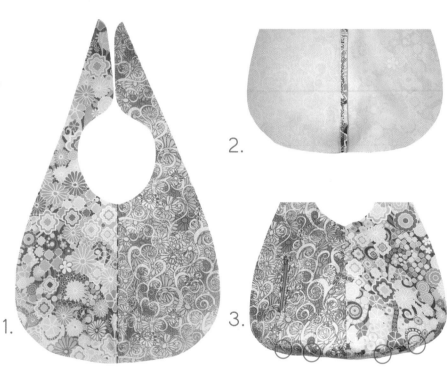

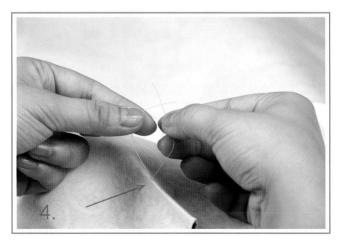

4. Leave a length of the sewing threads at the point of the darts and tie knots to secure the threads.

5. Press the darts in the same direction.

6. Put the 2 pieces of the Exterior Main Body right sides together with the dart seams abutting. Stitch the U shape and press the seam open.

6.

7. Put the 2 pieces of the Lining Upper Main Body right sides together and stitch the short straight edges. Press the seams open.

8. Use pins or clips to align the top edges of the Exterior Main Body with the Lining Upper Main Body and stitch.

Note: The leaf-shape part of the Lining Upper Main Body is slightly larger than the leaf-shape part of the Exterior Main Body. As a result, it is normal to have a ruffle at the leaf-shape part of the Lining Upper Main Body.

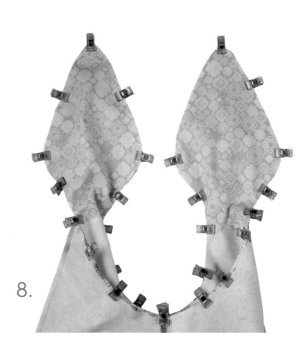

7.

8.

9. Clip and notch the curves. Turn right-side out and press.

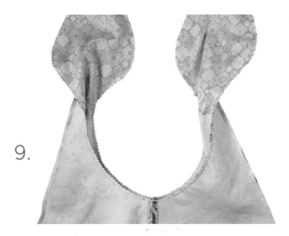

9.

10. Align the zipper tab with the closed-end of the zipper, right sides together, and stitch. Fold under a ¼" seam allowance along the edge of the opposite side of the tab.

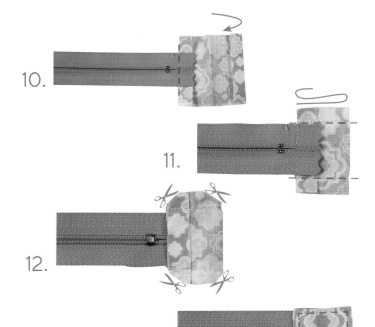

10.

11.

11. Fold the zipper tab in half, right sides together, and stitch the sides as shown.

12. Clip the corners.

12.

13. Turn the tab right-side out and topstitch ⅛" from the edges.

13.

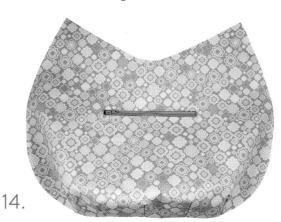

14.

14. Make pockets as desired on the Lining Lower Main Body. (Refer to the Zipper Pocket and Slip Pocket instructions, pages 5-6, 8.) Sew the lining darts as before.

15. Iron the darts in the same direction.

16. Put the 2 pieces of the Lining Lower Main Body right sides together, abutting the dart seams. Stitch the U shape, leaving an opening for turning later, and press the seam open.

15.

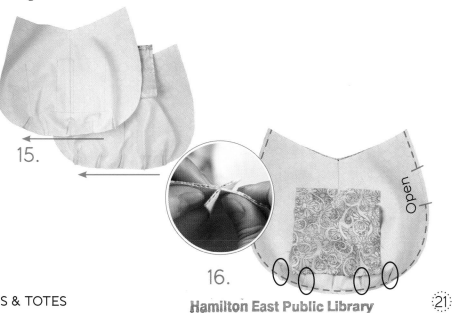

16.

open

17. Tape wash-away tape at the bottom edge of the Lining Upper Main Body. Leave about 1⅛" untaped.

18. Measure the length of the wash-away tape on the Lining Upper Main Body. Tape that exact length of tape along the wrong side of the zipper, starting at the opening end.

19. Put the zipper and the Lining Upper Main Body right sides together and tape the zipper at the bottom edge of the Lining Upper Main Body with the opening end toward the Lining Upper Main Body bottom edge seam. (By doing so, this end of the zipper will be sewn into the seam later on.) Put the closed end, starting from the untaped point to the zipper tab end, away from the Lining Upper Main Body bottom edge seam. (By doing so, you can avoid stitching to the zipper.)

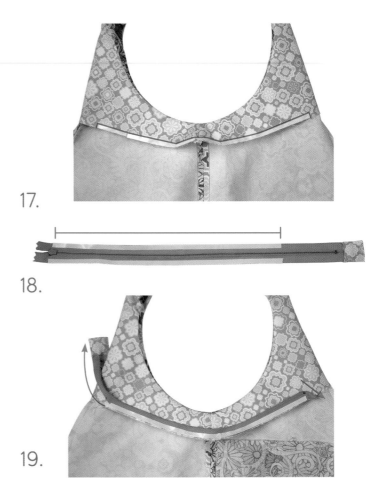

17.

18.

19.

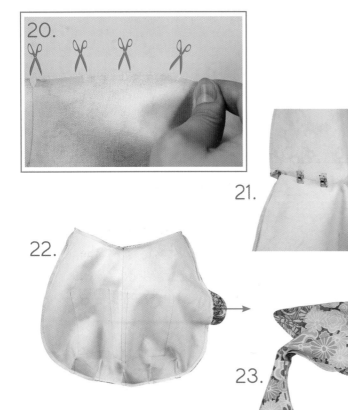

20.

21.

22.

23.

20. Clip the top edge of the Lining Lower Main Body in order to match the length of the bottom edge of the Lining Upper Main Body.

21. Use wash-away tape on the zipper, and clips or pins to match the bottom edge of the Lining Upper Main Body and the top edge of the Lining Lower Main Body. Stitch together.

22. Turn right-side out through the opening at the side of the lining.

23. Topstitch the top edge of the bag until the stop point of the heavyweight interfacing.

24. Iron heavyweight interfacing at the center wrong-side of the Shoulder Strap fabric.

24.

25. Fold the Shoulder Strap wrong-side out and stitch the long edge of the strap.

25.

26. Press and iron the seam open and center it on the strap.

26.

27.

27. Turn the strap right-side out and fold in the seam allowance on one short edge.

28. Use a bodkin to pull the low-loft polyester batting into the strap until it aligns with the heavyweight interfacing.

29. The area with heavyweight interfacing should be in the middle of the strap.

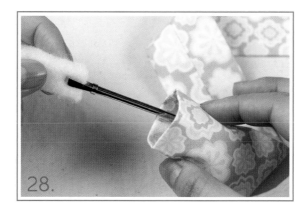

28.

30. Pass the rectangular rings through the 2 short ends of the strap and roughly position them at the ends of the batting.

29.

30.

31. Put the unfolded short end of the strap into the folded seam end of the strap.

32. Align the folded end with the center of the batting/heavyweight interfacing.

33. Stitch the strap to fasten the rings and batting.

34. Pass the leaf-shaped part of the Main Body through the rectangular rings between the rectangular ring position and the stop point of the heavyweight interfacing shown on the Lining Upper Main Body pattern. Fold the leaf-shaped part of the Main Body down. There will be the ruffle at this point. Shape it naturally. With the Exterior Main Body right sides together, align the rectangular ring with the stop point and stitch at the stop point to secure the rectangular ring.

Materials

- 1⅝" yard of woven fusible heavyweight interfacing
- ½ yard of woven fusible lightweight interfacing
- 1 yard of 1½" wide webbing
- Two ½" magnetic snap closures
- Two 6" zippers
- One 12" zipper
- Two 1" D-rings
- Fabric A – ⅞ yard
- Fabric B – ¾ yard
- Fabric C (lining) – ⅞ yard

Three-Layer Handbag

Cutting and Fusing Instructions

Fabric A		
Main Body	1 piece from the Exterior Main Body pattern	Iron with heavyweight interfacing.
Fabric B		
Exterior Pocket	2 pieces from the Exterior Pocket pattern	Iron with heavyweight interfacing.
Zipper Casing	2 pieces 12½" x 3½"	Iron with heavyweight interfacing.
Zipper Pocket	1 piece 7½" x 13½"*	Iron with lightweight interfacing.
D-ring loops	2 pieces 2½" x 2¼"	Iron with 1" x 2¼" heavyweight interfacing.

Fabric C (Lining)		
Main Body	1 piece from the Lining Main Body pattern	Iron with heavyweight interfacing.
Slip Pocket	1 piece 11" x 13"*	Iron with 11" x 6½" lightweight interfacing.
Zipper Pocket	1 piece 7½" x 13½"*	Iron with lightweight interfacing.
*Pocket sizes can be adjusted as preferred.		

Sewing Instructions

1. Mark the pleat positions on the Exterior Main Body according to the pattern.

> Note: The figure is only half of the Main Body pattern/fabric. Do both halves the same way.

2. Baste to secure the pleats.

1.

2.

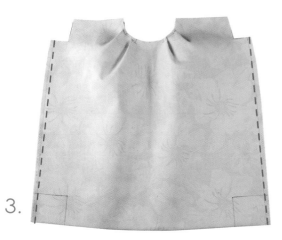

3. Fold the Exterior Main Body fabric in half, right sides together, and sew the sides.

4. Flatten the 2 bottom corners, mark 5" flat bottom lines, and sew the lines. Trim to ¼" seam allowance.

5. Make the pockets as desired on the Lining Main Body fabric, 2½" from the top with the 6" zippers. (Refer to the Zipper Pocket and Slip Pocket instructions, pages 5–6, 8.)

3.

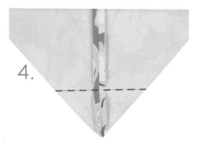

4.

5.

6.

7.

8.

9.

6. Use wash-away tape to make a three-layered zippy sandwich with the Lining Main Body right-side up on the bottom, the 12" zipper right-side up in the middle, and the Zipper Casing wrong-side up on top.

7. Stitch with a zipper foot.

8. Turn the 2 fabrics wrong sides together and topstitch, ⅛" from the edge. Repeat steps 6-8 to install the second side of the 12" zipper on the other side of the Lining Main Body.

9. Fold the Lining Main Body fabric in half, right sides together, and sew the sides.

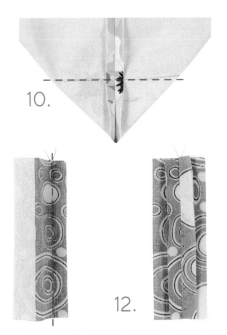

10.

11.   12.

10. Flatten the 2 bottom corners, mark 5" flat bottom lines, and stitch the lines. Trim to ¼" seam allowance.

11. Fold a D-ring loop in half lengthwise, right sides together, and stitch the long edge.

12. Press the seam open and iron to position the seam in the center.

13. Turn right-side out and topstitch, ⅛"
from the long edges.

14. Thread a D-ring through the loop, fold
the loop in half, and baste the short edge.
Repeat steps 11-14 to complete another
D-ring loop.

13.
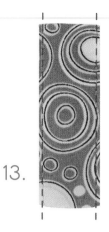

14.

15.

16.

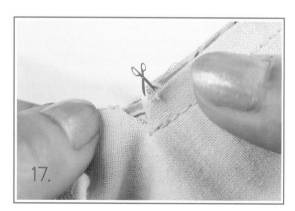
17.

15. Baste the 2 D-ring loops to the
center of the top edge side of the
Exterior Main Body.

16. Put the Exterior Main Body into
the Lining Main Body right sides
together, and sew the vertical line of
an L shape at the top edge on both
sides.

17. Clip the corner of the L shape.
Be careful not to cut the stitches.

18. Form the Zipper Casing fabric
into a shape like an isosceles triangle
and baste.

18.
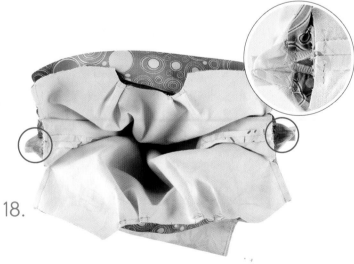
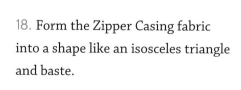
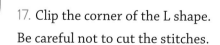

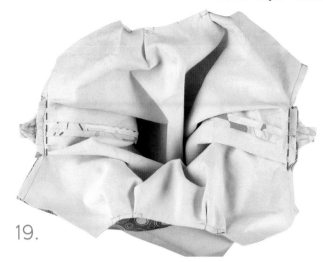

19. Align the horizontal line of the L shape with the bottom of the triangle and sew.

20. Make pockets as desired on the Exterior Pocket fabrics, 4" from the top. (Refer to the Zipper Pocket and Slip Pocket instructions, pages 5–6, 8.)

19.

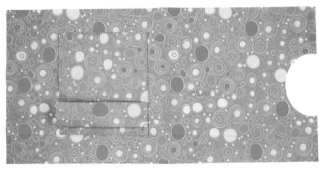

20.

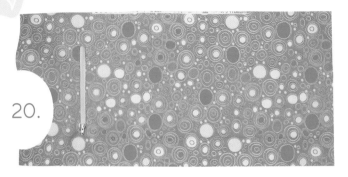

21.

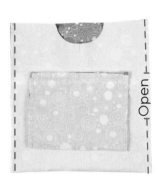

22.

21. Fold one Exterior Pocket fabric in half, right sides together, and sew the sides.

22. Fold another Exterior Pocket fabric in half, right sides together, and sew the sides. Leave an opening for turning at one side.

23. Cut the 1 yard webbing in half and baste the 2 webbing strips to the top edge of the Exterior Main Body. Adjust the length as you prefer.

23.

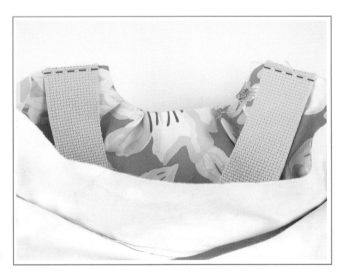

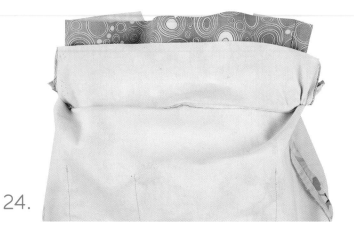

24.

24. Put the Exterior Pockets between the Exterior and Lining Main Body, right sides together.

25. Stitch the Exterior Pockets to the Main Body.

25.

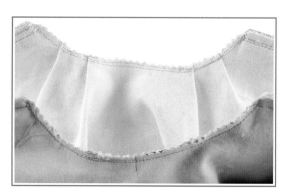

26.

26. Clip and notch the curves along the top edge.

27. Turn right-side out through the opening and shape the bag. Topstitch ¼" from the top edge.

28. Insert the magnetic snaps to the Exterior Pockets and close the opening.

27.

28.

Bags

Foldable Eco Bag

Fresh Shoulder Bag

Four-Piece Eco Bag

Spicy Girl Messenger Bag

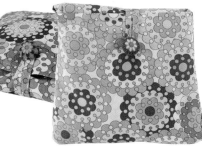

Materials

- Two 1" Self-Covered Buttons
- One 1¼" Self-Covered Button
- Fabric A – 1 yard
- Fabric B – ¾ yard

Foldable Eco Bag

Cutting and Fusing Instructions

All the cutting sizes include ¼" seam allowance.

Fabric A

Exterior Main Body	1 piece 28" x 17¼"
Lining Gusset	2 pieces from the Gusset pattern
Handles	2 pieces 6½" x 20"
Front Pocket	1 piece from the Front Pocket pattern (place on fold)
2 covers for 1" buttons	2 circles 1¾" diameter
1 cover for 1¼" button	1 circle 2¼" in diameter
Main Body Button Loop	1 strip 1½" x 9"
Front Pocket Button Loop	1 strip 1⅛" x 6¼"

Foldable Eco Bag features fabrics from Free Spirit Fabrics (http://freespiritfabric.com)

Fabric B	
Lining Main Body	1 piece 28" x 17¼"
Exterior Gusset	2 pieces from the Gusset pattern

Sewing Instructions

1. Fold the Handle fabric in half lengthwise, right sides together, and stitch the long edge.

1.

2. Press the seam open and iron to position the seam in the center.

2.

3. Turn right-side out and topstitch ⅛" from the long edges.

3.

4.

5.

4. Fold the Front Pocket fabric in half, wrong sides together, and stitch the U shape. Leave an opening along the bottom edge. Clip the round corners.

5. Turn right-side out through the opening. Press and shape the Front Pocket. Topstitch ³/₁₆" from the top edge.

6.

7.

6. Iron the long edges of both the Main Body Button Loop and Front Pocket Button Loop fabrics to the center.

7. Fold the Loop fabrics in half again and topstitch ⅛" from the long edges.

8. Put the Front Pocket 4" from the top edge of the Exterior Main Body fabric. Topstitch the U shape, ⅛" from the edge.

8.

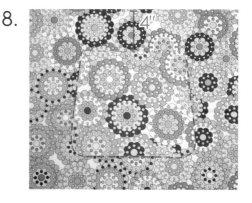

9. Mark the pleat positions on both top (short) edges of the Exterior Main Body fabric.

10. Baste the pleats in place.

11. With the short raw edges of the Front Pocket Button Loop pointing upwards, fold in half and position 3/16" below the center top edge of the pocket. Stitch ¼" from the short raw edges of the loop to the Exterior Main Body.

12. Flip the Front Pocket Button Loop up and stitch again at the edge of the Front Pocket.

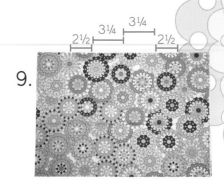

9.

10.

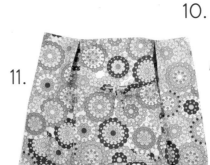

11.

12.

13.

14.

13. Make the pleats in the Exterior Gusset fabric according to the pattern.

14. Match a side (long) edge of the Exterior Main Body with the Exterior Gusset U-shape, right sides together, clipping the Exterior Main Body fabric to fit the curve of the Exterior Gusset. Stitch. Repeat with the second gusset on the other side of the Exterior Main Body.

15. That finishes the Exterior Main Body.

15.

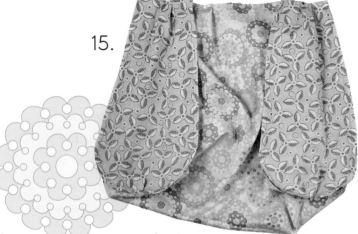

16. Follow steps 9 & 10 to secure the pleats of the Lining Main Body fabric.

16.

17.

17. Make the pleats of the Lining Gusset fabric according to the Gusset pattern.

18. Repeat step 14 to sew the Lining Gussets to the Lining Main Body, but leave an opening on one side for turning later.

18.

19.

19. That finishes the Lining Main Body.

20.

20. Position the handles with the edges of the Main Body Gussets, aligning the raw edges at the top. Baste the handles in place.

21.

22.

21. Fully insert the Lining Main Body right-side out into the Exterior Main Body wrong-side out and stitch the top edges together.

22. Turn the bag right-side out through the opening in the lining. Iron and shape the bag. Topstitch the top edge of the bag ¼" from the edge. Close the opening.

23. Fold the center part of the handles in thirds so they are about 1¼" wide. Zigzag stitch the center and edges of the folded handle 1¾" from the center in both directions. With the short raw edges of the Main Body Button Loop pointing upwards, fold in half. Position the loop at the topstitching line of the Back Exterior Main Body. Stitch the loop ¼" from the short raw edges.

23.

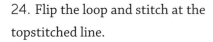

1¾" 1¾"

24. Flip the loop and stitch at the topstitched line.

24.

25. Follow the instructions to make 3 Self-Covered Buttons (page 9). Sew the 1¼" button on the Front Main Body and the 1" buttons on the inside and outside of the Front Pocket.

25.

26. Lay the bag pocket-side down, fold the bag to the size of the pocket, and turn the pocket inside-out, tucking the bag into the pocket as you go. Slip the Front Pocket Button Loop over the 1" button on the lining (now the outside) of the pocket.

26.

Materials

- 1¼ yards of woven fusible heavyweight interfacing
- ⅖ yard of woven fusible lightweight interfacing
- 28" of 1" wide webbing
- One ½" magnetic snap closure
- One 6" zipper
- Two ⅝" D-rings
- 19½" of ⅜" wide elastic
- Fabric A – ¾ yard
- Fabric B – ⅔ yard
- Stiffener – cut the size of the base (optional)

Fresh Shoulder Bag

Cutting and Fusing Instructions

Fabric A (Orange print)

Upper Main Body	4 pieces from the Upper Main Body pattern (2 Exterior, 2 Lining)	Iron with heavyweight interfacing.
Base	1 piece from the Base pattern (Exterior)	Iron with heavyweight interfacing.
Magnetic Snap Tab	2 pieces from the Magnetic Snap Tab pattern	Iron with heavyweight interfacing excluding seam allowance.
Decorative Strip for Webbing	2 strips 1" x 14"	You may adjust the length of the fabric based on the length of the webbing.

Fabric B (White background print)		
Exterior Lower Main Body	2 pieces from the Lower Main Body pattern	Iron with heavyweight interfacing.
Decorative Strip for Upper Main Body	4 strips 1" x 5½"	
Decorative Strip for Magnetic Snap Tab	1 strip 1" x 5"	
Fabric C (Lining)		
Lower Main Body	2 pieces from the Lower Main Body pattern	Iron with heavyweight interfacing.
Base	1 piece from the Base pattern	Iron with heavyweight interfacing.
Zipper Pocket	1 piece 7½" x 13½"*	Iron with lightweight interfacing.
Elasticized Pocket	1 piece 23½" x 12"*	Iron with 23½" x 6" lightweight interfacing.

*Pocket sizes can be adjusted as preferred.

Sewing Instructions

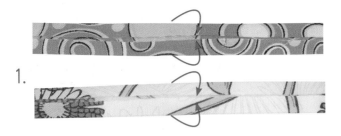

1.

2.

1. Fold the long edges of all Decorative Strips to the center and press.

2. Mark a straight line across the center of the 2 Exterior Upper Main Body pieces.

3. Align the center of a Decorative Strip for Upper Main Body with the left half of the marked line. Topstitch the Decorative Strip, ⅛" from the right-side edge. When the stitching reaches about 2" from the center of the Upper Main Body, thread the Decorative Strip through the D-ring and fold the seam allowance between the Decorative Strip and the Upper Main Body. Stitch across and back to form a rectangle of stitches.

3.

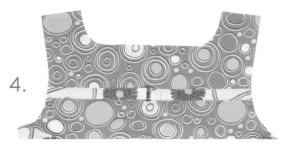

4.

4. Follow the previous step to stitch the right side of the Decorative Strip.

5. Repeat steps 2-4 to stitch the other Decorative Strip to the other Exterior Upper Main Body.

5.

6.

7.

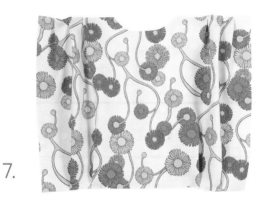

6. Mark the pleat positions on the Exterior Lower Main Body pieces according to the pattern.

7. Baste to secure the pleats.

8. Put 2 Exterior Lower Main Body fabrics right sides together and stitch the sides. Press the seams open.

9. Align the bottom-center of the Exterior Upper Main Body fabrics with the side seams of the Exterior Lower Main Body, right sides together. Use clips or pins to grip the fabrics.

10. Stitch the Exterior Upper Main Body fabrics to the Exterior Lower Main Body.

8.

9.

10.

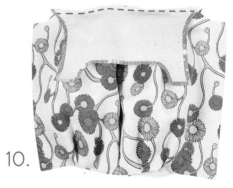

11.

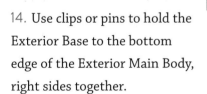

12.

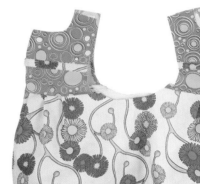

13.

11. When finished, the front view of the Exterior Main Body should look like this.

12. Flip the right side of the Exterior Upper Main Body up and press the seam allowance toward the Exterior Upper Main Body. Topstitch on the Exterior Upper Main Body, ⅛" from the seam.

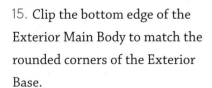

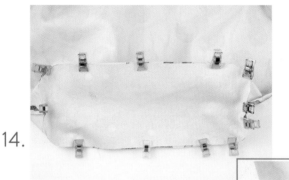

14.

15.

13. When finished, the front view of the Exterior Main Body should look like this.

14. Use clips or pins to hold the Exterior Base to the bottom edge of the Exterior Main Body, right sides together.

15. Clip the bottom edge of the Exterior Main Body to match the rounded corners of the Exterior Base.

16. Stitch the Exterior Base to the Exterior Main Body.

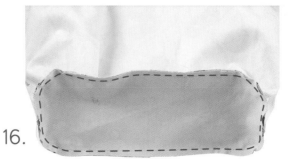

16.

17. Take one piece of the Magnetic Snap Tab fabric and mark a line in the center.

18. Align the center of the Decorative Strip for the Magnetic Snap Tab with the marked line. Topstitch onto the Decorative Strip, ⅛" from the side edge.

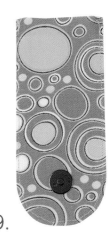

17.　　　　18.　　　　19.

19. Apply the non-magnetic part of the magnetic snap to the second Magnetic Snap Tab piece.

20. Position the 2 Magnetic Snap Tab fabrics right sides together and stitch the U shape.

21. Notch or pink the curves.

22. Turn right-side out, press, and topstitch the Magnetic Snap Tab ⅛" from the side edge.

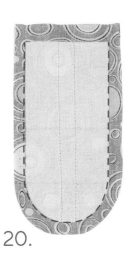

20.　　　　21.　　　　22.

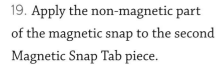

23.

23. Cut the webbing in half, center the Decorative Strip on the webbing, and topstitch in place, ⅛" from the side edge.

Note: You can adjust the length of the webbing, but any shorter than indicated will make it difficult to sew the bag Exterior and Lining together (Step 33).

24. Repeat steps 6 & 7 to baste the pleats of the Lining Lower Main Body fabrics.

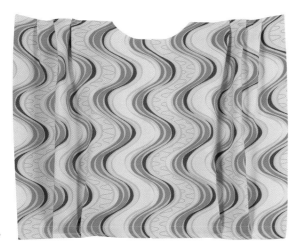

24.

25. Make pockets as you prefer on the two Lining Lower Main Body fabrics. (Refer to the Zipper Pocket and Elasticized Pocket instructions, pages 5-7.) With the right sides together, stitch the lining sides, leaving an opening for turning later.

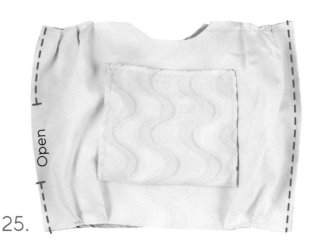

25.

26. Align the bottom center of the Lining Upper Main Body pieces with the side seams of the Lining Lower Main Body, right sides together, and stitch.

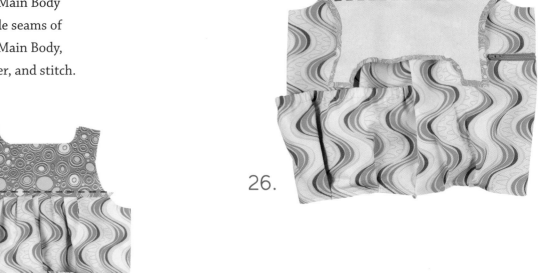

26.

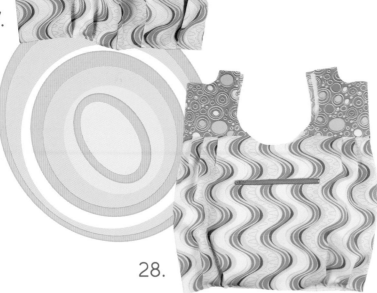

27.

28.

27. Flip the right side of the Lining Upper Main Body up and press the seam allowance toward the Lining Upper Main Body. Topstitch on the Lining Upper Main Body, ⅛" from the seam.

28. The front view of the Lining Main Body should look like this.

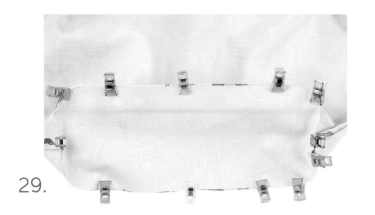

29.

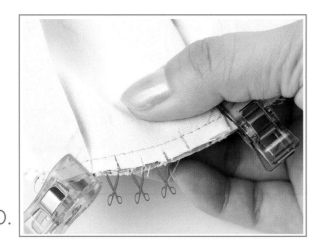

30.

29. Use clips or pins to hold the Lining Base to the bottom edge of the Lining Main Body, right sides together.

30. Clip the bottom edge of the Lining Main Body to match the rounded corners of the Lining Base.

31.

31. Stitch the Lining Base to the Lining Main Body.

32. Baste the webbing and Magnetic Snap Tab at the top edge of the Exterior Main Body.

32.

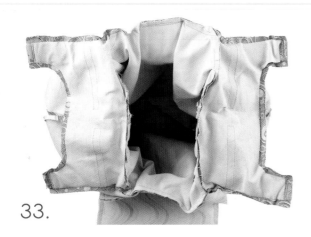

33.

33. Fully insert the Exterior Main Body right-side out into the Lining Main Body wrong-side out. Stitch the top edges together.

34. Clip and notch the curves and corners.

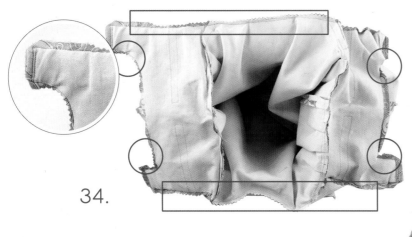

34.

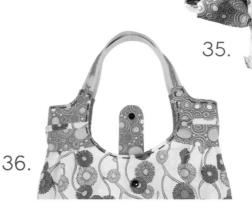

35.

35. Turn right-side out through the opening.

36. Topstitch ³/₁₆" from the top edge. Apply the magnetic part of the magnetic snap closure to the front Main Body.

36.

37. You may choose to insert PE board at the bottom through the opening. Iron and shape the bag. Close the opening.

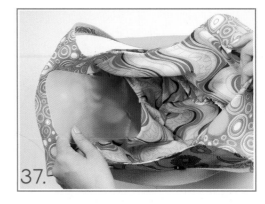

37.

Materials

- One 1¼" Self-Covered Button
- Fabric A – 1⅓ yards
- Fabric B –1⅓ yards

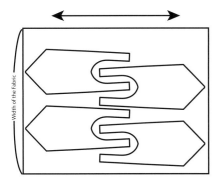

Cutting Layout

Four-Piece Eco Bag

Cutting and Fusing Instructions

All the cutting sizes include ¼" seam allowance.

Fabric A		
Exterior Main Body	2 pieces from the Main Body pattern	Iron with heavyweight interfacing.
Lining Main Body	2 pieces from the Main Body pattern	

Fabric B		
Exterior Main Body	2 pieces from the Main Body pattern	Iron with heavyweight interfacing.
Lining Main Body	2 pieces from the Main Body pattern	
Button Loop	1 strip 1½" x 10"	
Ties	2 strips 1½" x 12"	
1¼" Self-Covered Button fabric	1 circle 2¼" in diameter	

Sewing Instructions

1. Place one Fabric A Exterior Main Body piece and one Fabric B Exterior Main Body piece right sides together and stitch one side and bottom edge. Repeat with the other 2 pieces of Exterior Main Body.

2. Open the 2 sets of Exterior Main Body. With right sides together, stitch the sides and bottom.

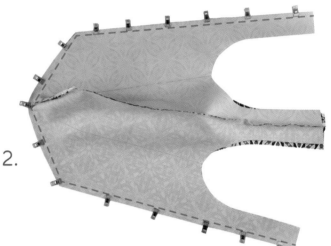

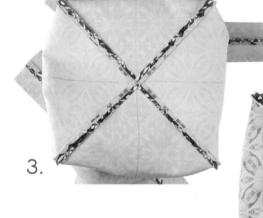

3. Press the seams open.

4. Repeat steps 1–3 with the 4 Lining Main Body pieces.

5. Pass the Button Loop and Tie fabric through a tape maker and iron the folds.

6. Iron the Button Loop and Tie fabric in half lengthwise and topstitch ⅛" from the long edges.

7.

7. Choose 2 opposite sides of the Exterior Main Body as the Bag Gusset. Baste the ties at the top center edge of the gusset. Fold the Button Loop in half and baste the short raw edges of the Button Loop at the top center edge of the Back Main Body.

8. Fully insert the Lining Main Body right-side out into the Exterior Main Body wrong-side out. Stitch the top edges and the handle edges together as shown. Leave open at the top and inside edges of the handles.

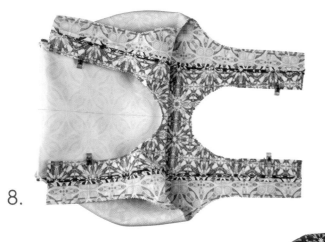

8.

9. Turn right-side out through one of the openings.

10. With the short edges of the Front Main Body Handle right sides together, and the short edges of the Back Main Body Handle right sides together, stitch the short edges.

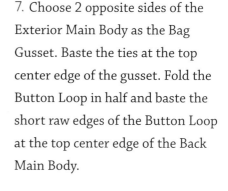

9.

10.

11. Turn the handles right-side out, fold the openings seam in, and topstitch ⅛" from the handle and top edges of the bag.

11.

12. Fold in the long edges of the handles to meet in the center. Stitch a rectangle along the folded edges on both sides of the center seam.

12.

2⅜" 2⅜"

13. Cover the button (see Self-Covered Button instructions, page 9).

13.

14. Sew the button on the front Main Body to align with the loop.

14.

Materials

- 1⅛ yards of woven fusible heavyweight interfacing
- ⅔ yard of woven fusible lightweight interfacing
- One 5" zipper
- Two 7" zippers
- One 14" zipper
- One 1½" rectangular ring
- One 1½" strap slider
- Three ¾" magnetic snap closures
- 1⅔ yards of 1½" wide webbing
- Fabric A – ¾ yard
- Fabric B –½ yard
- Fabric C (Lining) – ¾ yard

Spicy Girl Messenger Bag

Cutting and Fusing Instructions

Fabric A		
Main Body	1 piece from the Main Body pattern	Iron with heavyweight interfacing.
Front Pocket	1 piece 14½" x 6¾"	Iron with heavyweight interfacing without seam allowance.
Back Zipper Pocket	1 piece 8½" x 14¼"	Iron with lightweight interfacing.
Zipper Tab	1 piece 2" x 2¾"	

Fabric B		
Flap	2 mirror-image pieces from the Flap pattern	Iron the exterior Flap with heavyweight interfacing.
Decorative Base	1 piece from the Decorative Base pattern	Iron with heavyweight interfacing without seam allowance.
Flap Zipper Pocket	1 piece 6½" x 10"	Iron with lightweight interfacing.
Magnetic Snap Tab	1 piece 3¼" x 3"	Iron with 1⅛" x 2" heavyweight interfacing.
Zipper Casings	2 pieces 2³⁄₁₆" x 10⅜"	Iron with heavyweight interfacing without seam allowance.
Fabric C (Lining)		
Main Body	1 piece 17⅜" x 24½"	Iron with heavyweight interfacing.
Front Pocket	1 piece 14½" x 6¾"	Iron with lightweight interfacing.
Slip Pocket	1 piece 9" x 12"*	Iron with 9" x 6" lightweight interfacing.
Zipper Pocket	1 piece 8½" x 14¼"*	Iron with lightweight interfacing.
Zipper Casings	2 pieces 2³⁄₁₆" x 10⅝"	Iron with lightweight interfacing.

*Pocket sizes can be adjusted as preferred.

Sewing Instructions

1. Put the Exterior and Lining Front Pocket fabrics right sides together and stitch the top edge.

1.

2. Iron the seam toward the Lining Front Pocket fabric and topstitch the fabric ⅛" from the stitched line.

2.

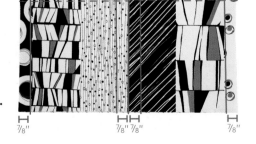

4.

3.

3. Put the Exterior and Lining Front Pocket fabrics right sides together again and stitch the sides. Clip the two top corners.

4. Turn the Front Pocket right-side out and iron to flatten. Topstitch ¼" from the top edge. Mark the fold lines of the Front Pocket.

5. Iron and fold the Front Pockets and topstitch ⅛" along the folds.

5.

6. Apply the magnetic snap closures to the Front Pocket with one magnetic part to the Exterior Front Pocket, 1½" from the bottom edge center of the left-side pocket, and the two non-magnetic parts to the Lining Front Pocket, 1" from the top edge.

6.

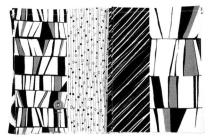

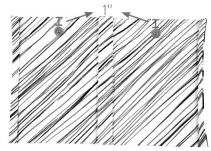

1½"

3½"

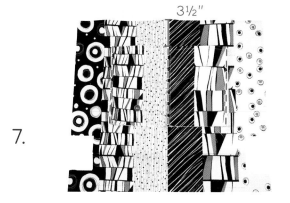

7.

7. Position the Front Pocket on the Exterior Main Body fabric 3½" from the top edge. Stitch the center and sides to make 2 Front Pockets.

8. Clip the outside corners of the Decorative Base fabric, then fold and iron the seam allowance to the wrong side of the fabric.

9. Align the Decorative Base fabric with the Exterior Main Body base area. Topstitch the Decorative Base fabric ⅛" from the folded seam allowance edges.

10. Apply two magnetic parts of the magnetic snap to the Exterior Main Body, aligning them with the two non-magnetic parts of the magnetic snap on the Lining Front Pocket.

8.

9.

10.

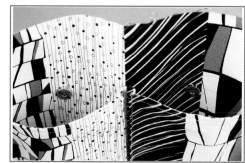

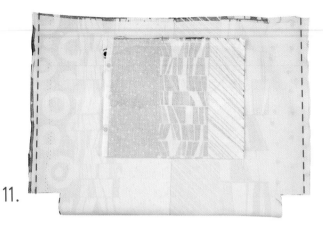

11.

11. Make a 7" zipper pocket in the Exterior Back. (Refer to the Zipper Pocket instructions, pages 5-6.) Fold the Exterior Main Body fabric in half, right sides together, and stitch the sides.

12. Press the seam open and stitch the flat bottom.

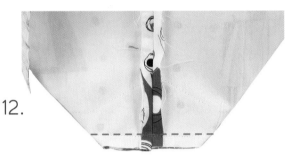

12.

13. Make the pockets as desired on the Lining Main Body fabric. (Refer to the Zipper Pocket and Slip Pocket instructions, pages 5-6, 8.)

14. Fold the Lining Main Body fabric in half, right sides together, and stitch the sides. Leave an opening at one side for turning later.

15. Stitch a flat bottom 4" long. Trim to ¼" seam allowance.

16. Iron a 1⅛" x 2" piece of heavyweight interfacing on the wrong side of the Magnetic Snap Tab.

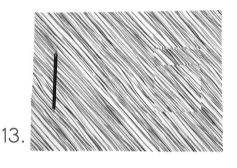

13.

14. Open

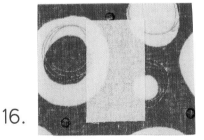

15.

4"

16.

17. Fold the Magnetic Snap Tab fabric in half, right sides together, and stitch.

18. Iron the seam to the center and stitch the bottom edge. Clip the bottom corners.

19. Turn the Magnetic Snap Tab fabric right-side out. Apply the last non-magnetic part of the magnetic snap to the Magnetic Snap Tab. Topstitch ⅛" from the edge.

17.    **18.** 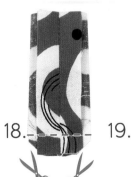   **19.**

20. Make a Zipper Pocket, positioning it according to the Flap pattern. (Refer to the Zipper Pocket instructions, pages 5-6.)

21. Baste the Magnetic Snap Tab onto the Exterior Flap.

22. Put the Exterior and Lining Flap right sides together and stitch 3 sides, leaving the top open. Clip the corners.

20.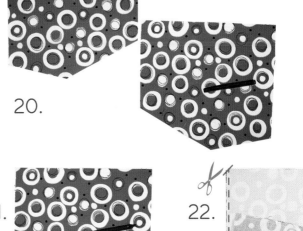

21.

22.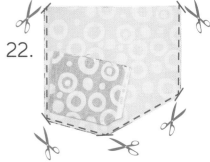

23. Turn right-side out through the top and topstitch ⅛" from the stitched edges.

24. Align the zipper tab with the closed-end of the zipper, right sides together, and stitch.

25. Fold the seam along the opposite side of the zipper tab. Fold the zipper tab in half and stitch the side edges as shown. Clip the corners.

26. Turn right-side out and topstitch the zipper tab, ⅛" from the edge.

27. Iron the seam allowance of one short edge toward the wrong side of the Exterior and Lining Zipper Casing fabrics.

28. Use wash-away tape to make a three-layered zippy sandwich with the Lining Zipper Casing right-side up on the bottom, the zipper right-side up in the middle, and the Exterior Zipper Casing fabric wrong-side up on the top.

23.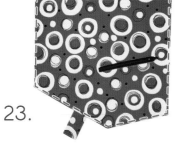

24.

25.

26.

27.

28.

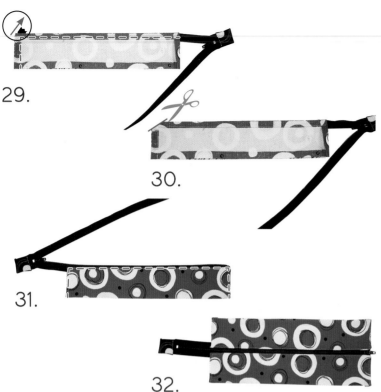

29.

30.

31.

32.

29. Fold back the end of the zipper-fabric to the outside of the Zipper Casing and use a zipper foot to stitch the L shape.

30. Clip the corner, trimming the Zipper and Casing fabric.

31. Turn the Zipper Casing right side out and press. Topstitch the L shape ⅛" from the edge.

32. Repeat steps 27-31 to finish the other Zipper Casing.

33. Cut a 3" piece of webbing. Thread the rectangular ring with the webbing. Fold the webbing in half and baste the short edges together.

34. Pass one end of the rest of the long webbing through the center bar of the strap slider. Fold in about ½" between the webbing and stitch. Thread the other end of the webbing through the rectangular ring and the strap slider.

35. Baste the Zipper Casings, the short edge of the long webbing, and basted short edge of the short webbing on the top edge of the Exterior Main Body.

36. Fully insert the Lining Main Body right-side out into the Exterior Main Body wrong-side out. Stitch the top edges together.

33.

34.

35.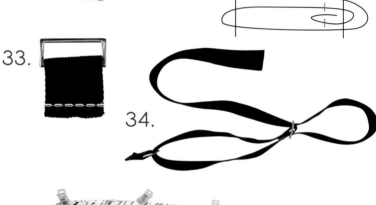

36.

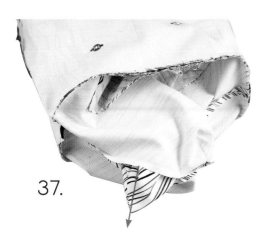

37.

37. Turn right-side out through the opening in the lining.

38. Topstitch 3/16" from the Main Body top edge.

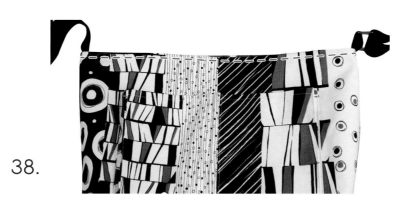

38.

39. Put the Flap and the Exterior Back Main Body exterior right sides together. Position the Flap 1¼" from the top edge of the Main Body, and stitch the Flap to the Exterior Back Main Body, 3/16" from the top edge of the Flap. Be careful NOT to stitch the Zipper Casing.

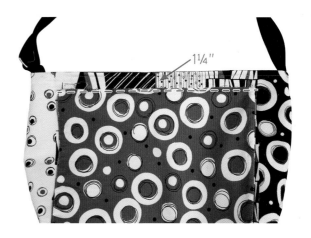

39.

40. Flip the Flap up and topstitch ½" from the stitched edge to complete the bag. Be careful NOT to stitch the Zipper Casing.

40.

Totes

Materials

- 1 1/6 yards of woven fusible heavyweight interfacing

- 2/5 yard of woven fusible lightweight interfacing

- 2 2/3 yards of 1" fusible waistband interfacing

- One 18" closed-end two-slider zip

- Three 6" zippers

- Two 1" rectangular rings

- Two 1" strap sliders

- Bag bottom stiffener 6" x 9½"

- Fabric A – ½ yard

- Fabric B – ¾ yard

- Fabric C (Lining) – 1 yard

Cutie Backpack

Cutting and Fusing Instructions

Fabric A		
Main Body	2 pieces from the Main Body pattern	Iron with heavyweight interfacing.
Exterior Back Zipper Pocket	1 piece 7½" x 14"	Iron with lightweight interfacing.
Fabric B		
Front Zipper Pocket	2 mirror-image pieces from the Front Pocket pattern	Iron ONE with heavyweight interfacing for the Exterior of the Front Pocket.
Upper Gusset	4 pieces from the Upper Gusset pattern	Iron TWO pieces with heavyweight interfacing for the Exterior of the Upper Gusset.

Fabric B		
Lower Gusset	4 pieces from the Lower Gusset pattern	Iron TWO pieces with heavyweight interfacing for the Exterior of the Lower Gusset.
Base	1 piece from the Base pattern	Iron with heavyweight interfacing.
Adjustable Straps	2 strips 3" x 38½"	Iron with 1" x 37½" waistband interfacing.**
Handles	2 strips 3" x 7⅞"	Iron with 1" x 6⅞" waistband interfacing.**
Rectangular Ring Loops	2 pieces 3" x 3¼"	Iron with 1" x 2¼" waistband interfacing.**
Fabric C (Lining)		
Main Body	2 pieces from the Main Body pattern	Iron with heavyweight interfacing.
Base	1 piece from the Base pattern	
Bottom Stiffener Cover	1 piece from the Base pattern	
Front Zipper Pocket Binding	1 bias-cut strip 1½" x 15¾"	
Base Binding	1 bias-cut strip 1½" x 39⅜"	
Zipper Pocket	1 piece 7½" x 14"	Iron with lightweight interfacing.
Slip Pocket	1 piece 9½" x 12½"	Iron with 9½" x 6¼" lightweight interfacing.

*Pocket sizes can be adjusted as preferred.
**Position the waistband interfacing edge along the center of the fabric. (See photo 10, page 60.)

Sewing Instructions

1. Stitch the long straight sides of the Exterior and Lining Front Zipper Pocket, right sides together.

2. Turn right-side out.

3. Pass the Front Zipper Pocket Binding fabric through a tape maker to iron the folds. Place the Front Zipper Pocket Binding right sides together with the left curved edge of the Exterior Front Zipper Pocket fabric and stitch.

1.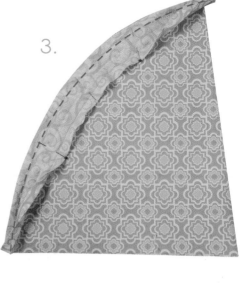

2.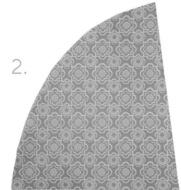

3.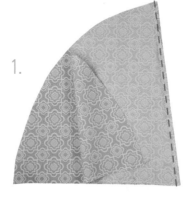

4.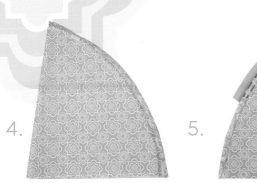

5.

4. Fold the binding to the Lining Front Zipper Pocket fabric. Use wash-away tape to position the binding on the Lining Front Zipper Pocket fabric.

5. Use wash-away tape to position one long edge of a 6" zipper, opening side up, on the curved edge, about 2" away from the top. Use a zipper foot to topstitch the binding to the zipper ⅛" from the teeth and lower edge of the binding.

6.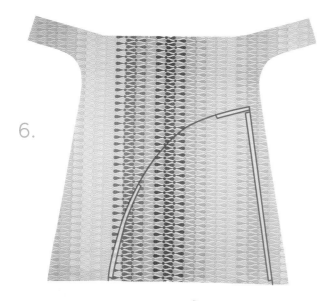

6. Mark the Front Zipper Pocket position on one piece of Exterior Main Body fabric according to the Main Body pattern (this will be the Exterior Front Main Body). Place wash-away tape along the marked curved edge, except where the zipper will be stitched.

7.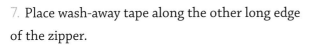

7. Place wash-away tape along the other long edge of the zipper.

8. Open the zipper and align the teeth with the marked curved line on the Exterior Front Main Body. Tape the zipper to the Exterior Front Main Body. Use a zipper foot to topstitch the zipper, ⅛" from the long and teeth edge.

8.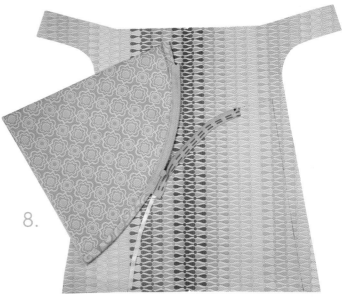

9. Turn the Lining Front Zipper Pocket right sides together with the Exterior Front Main Body. Topstitch the Front Zipper Pocket as shown.

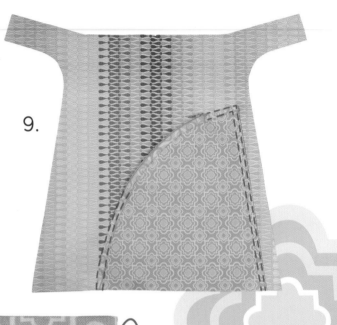

10. Fold and press ½" seam allowances on the long edges of the Adjustable Straps, Handles, and Rectangular Ring Loops.

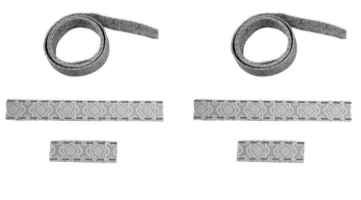

11. Fold the 2 Adjustable Straps, 2 Handles, and 2 Rectangular Ring Loops in half lengthwise and press. Topstitch ⅛" from the long edges.

12. Thread the rectangular rings with the loops, fold the loops in half, and baste the short edges together.

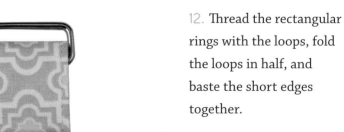

13. Thread one end of the Adjustable Strap through the center bar of the strap slider. Fold the seam between the strap and stitch. Thread the other end of the strap through the rectangular ring and the strap slider to finish the strap. Repeat to finish the second strap.

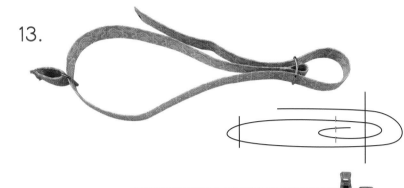

13.

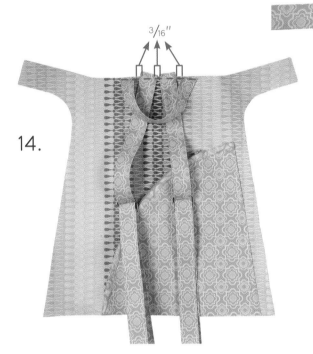

14.

$3/16''$

14. Baste the 2 Adjustable Straps and 2 short ends of one handle to the top edge of the Exterior Front Main Body about $3/16''$ apart.

Note: The front of the Adjustable Straps MUST face the right side of the Exterior Front Main Body.

15. Put the short edges of the Exterior Front Main Body right sides together and stitch. Press the seam open.

16. Center the seam on the Exterior Front Main Body. Align the top edges, right sides together, and stitch. Trim the 2 corners, being careful NOT to cut the stitching.

15.

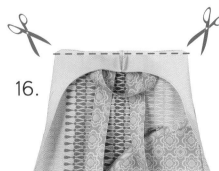

16.

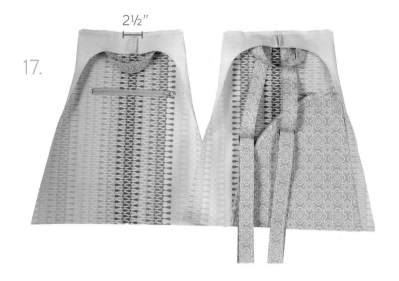

17.

2½"

18.

17. Make the Exterior Back 6" Zipper Pocket on the Exterior Back Main Body. (Refer to the Zipper Pocket instructions, page 5-6.) Baste the 2 short ends of the other handle. Repeat steps 15 & 16 to make the Exterior Back Main Body.

18. Use wash-away tape to make a three-layered zippy sandwich with the Lining Upper Gusset right-side up on the bottom, the 18" zipper right-side up in the middle, and the Exterior Upper Gusset wrong-side up on the top. Match the long edge of the zipper with the Stitching Zipper edge, shown on the Upper Gusset pattern.

19. Use a zipper foot to stitch the 3 layers together.

20. Turn right-side out. Match the Exterior Upper Gusset with the Lining Upper Gusset and topstitch the Upper Gusset ⅛" from the straight edge.

21. Repeat steps 18–20 to stitch the Upper Gusset to the other long edge of the zipper.

19.

20.

21.

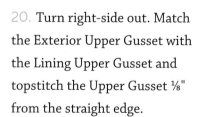

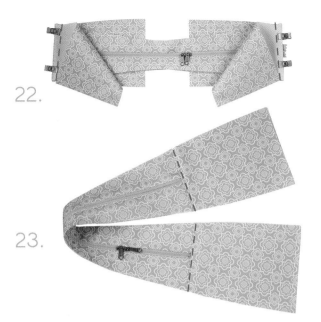

22.

23.

22. Layer the Lining Lower Gusset right-side up on the bottom, Exterior Upper Zipper Gusset right-side up in the middle, and Exterior Lower Gusset wrong-side up on the top. Match the short edges of the Lower Gusset with the short edges of the Upper Zipper Gusset and stitch.

23. Turn right-side out and topstitch the Lower Gusset ⅛" from the stitched line. The Gusset is ready to use.

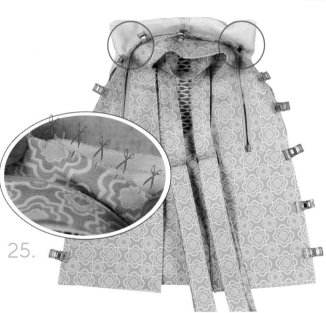

24.

24. Make the pockets on the Lining Main Body fabric. Use a 6" zipper. (Refer to the Zipper Pocket and Slip Pocket instructions, pages 5–6, 8.) Repeat Steps 15 & 16 to make the Lining Main Body.

25. Clip the top curved edge of the Exterior Front Main Body in order to match the long edge of the Gusset. Use clips or pins to hold the Gusset to the Exterior Front Main Body, exterior right sides together.

25.

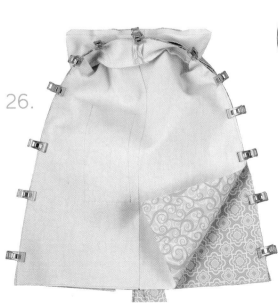

26.

26. Take one piece of the Lining Main Body fabric wrong-side out to match the Exterior Front Main Body. Clip or pin all 3 layers together.

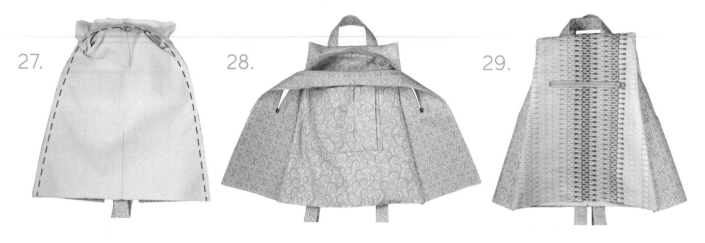

27.

28.

29.

30.

27. Stitch as shown.

28. Turn right-side out to finish the Front Main Body.

29. Repeat steps 25–28 to finish the Back Main Body.

30. Thread the Adjustable Straps through the handle on the Back Main Body.

31. Baste the Rectangular Ring Loops on the bottom edge of the Back Main Body 1½" from the sides.

31.

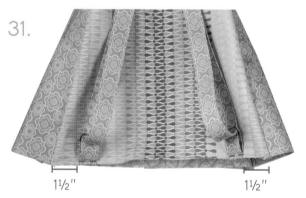

1½"

1½"

32. Fold the short-edge seam allowance of the PE Board Cover.

33. Topstitch the short edge of the PE Board Cover ³⁄₁₆".

32.

33.

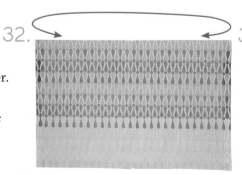

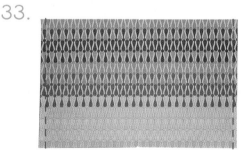

34.

34. Layer the Exterior Base wrong-side up on the bottom, the Lining Base right-side up in the middle, and PE Board Cover right-side up on top.

35. Baste around the edges of the layers to finish the base.

35.

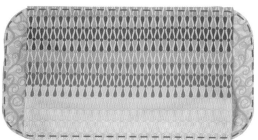

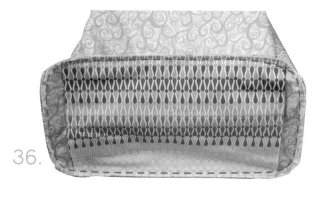

36.

37.

36. Match the bottom edge of the Main Body with the Base Exterior fabric, right sides together.

37. Pass the Base Binding fabric through a tape maker to iron the folds. With the Base Binding and the bottom edge of the Lining Main Body right sides together, stitch around the base.

38. Fold the Base Binding to the Lining Base and topstitch $1/16$" on the binding to finish the bag.

39. Turn the exterior right-side out. Insert stiffener cut to the size of the base between the Lining Base and Cover fabric.

38.

39.

Materials

- 1⅔ yards of woven fusible heavyweight interfacing
- ¾ yard woven fusible lightweight interfacing
- ¾ yard of 1" fusible waistband interfacing
- Four 4" zippers (for Exterior Front/Back Zipper Pockets)
- One 8" zipper (for Lining Zipper Pocket)
- Two 9" zippers (for Side Zipper Pockets)
- One 14" zipper (for Main Body)
- One 27" closed-end two-slider zipper (for Extension)
- 1 yard of 1½" wide webbing
- Fabric A (Orange print) – ⅞ yard
- Fabric B (Green print) – ⅞ yard
- Fabric C (Black) – ½ yard
- Fabric D (Lining) – ⅞ yard

Expandable Zipper Tote Bag features fabrics from Andover Fabrics™ (www.andoverfabrics.com)

Expandable Zipper Tote Bag

Cutting and Fusing Instructions

Fabric A (Orange print)

Main Body	1 piece 8" x 27½"	Iron with heavyweight interfacing.
Zipper Casings	2 pieces from the Zipper Casing pattern	Iron with heavyweight interfacing.
Zipper Tabs	4 strips 1" x 1½"	
Front and Back 4" Zipper Pockets	2 pieces 5½" x 11"	Iron with lightweight interfacing.
9" Side Zipper Pocket	1 piece 10½" x 11"	Iron with lightweight interfacing.
Extension Decorative Strip	1 piece 2" x 27½"	Iron with 1" x 27" waistband interfacing.

Fabric B (Green print)		
Main Body	1 piece 8" x 27½"	Iron with heavyweight interfacing.
Front and Back 4" Zipper Pockets	2 pieces 5½" x 11"	Iron with lightweight interfacing.
Side 9" Zipper Pocket	1 piece 10½" x 11"	Iron with lightweight interfacing.
Fabric C (Black)		
Extension	1 piece 3⅛" x 27½"	
Zipper Extension Decorative Strips	2 strips 1⅜" x 29½"	
Main Body Decorative Strip	1 strip 2" x 31¾"	
Main Body Binding	1 bias-cut strip 1½" x 31¾"	
Zipper Casing Binding	2 bias-cut strips 1½" x 8"	
Fabric D (Lining)		
Main Body	1 piece from the Lining Main Body pattern	Iron with heavyweight interfacing.
Zipper Casings	2 pieces from the Zipper Casing pattern	Iron with heavyweight interfacing.
Slip Pocket	1 piece 11" x 12"*	Iron with 11" x 6" lightweight interfacing.
8" Zipper Pocket	1 piece 9½" x 13½"*	Iron with lightweight interfacing.

*Pocket sizes can be adjusted as preferred.

Sewing Instructions

1. Make the Front and Back 4" Zipper Pockets on the 2 pieces of the Exterior Main Body fabric (pages 5–6).

1.

2.

3.

2. Iron the waistband interfacing in the middle of the Extension Decorative Strip.

3. Iron the long edges of the Extension Decorative Strip in toward the center.

4.

5.

6.

7.

4. Mark the center line on the right side of the Extension fabric.

5. Match the center of the Extension Decorative Strip with the marked center line on the Extension fabric and topstitch in place ⅛" from the long edges.

6. Align the long edge that is 1⅜" from the Front and Back 4" Zipper Pockets side of the Exterior Main Body with a long edge of the Zipper Extension Decorative Strip, right sides together, and stitch.

7. Fold and press the Zipper Extension Decorative Strip to the wrong side of the Exterior Main Body. (There is no need to fold the raw edge in.)

8. Repeat steps 6 & 7 to make the other Zipper Extension Decorative Strip and the other Exterior Main Body fabric.

8.

9. With the Extension and closed-end two-slider zipper right-side up, match the long edge and stitch.

9.

10. With one of the Exterior Main Body fabrics right-side up, place the long edge with the Zipper Extension Decorative Strip on top of the zipper. The edge should be close to the zipper teeth. Topstitch the Zipper Extension Decorative Strip ⅛" from the long edges.

10.

11. With the Extension and closed-end two-slider zipper right-side up, match the other long edge and stitch.

11.

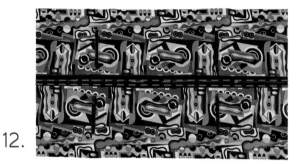

12.

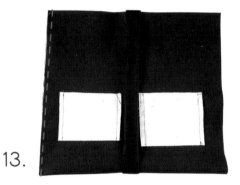

13.

12. With the other Exterior Main Body fabric right-side up, place the long edge with the Zipper Extension Decorative Strip on top of the zipper. The edge should be close to the zipper teeth. Topstitch the Zipper Extension Decorative Strip ⅛" from the long edges.

13. Fold the Exterior Main Body in half lengthwise, right sides together, and stitch one side.

14.

14. Using the stitched side as the center, make a Side 9" Zipper Pocket (pages 5-6) 3½" from the top edge.

15. Fold the Exterior Main Body in half again, right sides together, and stitch the other side.

15.

16.

16. Using the stitched side as the center, make another Side 9" Zipper Pocket (pages 5-6) 3½" from the top edge.

17. Flatten the 2 bottom corners, mark 4" flat bottom lines, and stitch on the marked lines. Trim to a ¼" seam allowance.

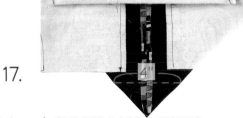

17.

18. Turn the Exterior Main Body right-side out. Cut the webbing in half and baste the raw edges along the top edge of the Exterior Main Body, 2½" from the center.

19. With the short edges of the Main Body Decorative Strip right sides together, stitch the short edges together. Press the seam open.

20. With the Exterior Main Body and the Main Body Decorative Strip right sides together, stitch the top edge of the Exterior Main Body with one long edge of the Main Body Decorative Strip.

21. Turn the Main Body Decorative Strip right-side out and flip the webbing up. Topstitch on the Main Body Decorative Strip ⅛" from the bottom edge.

18. 2½"

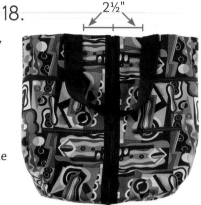

19.

20.

21.

22.

23.

24.

25.

26.

27.

22. Place the short edges of the 14" zipper between 2 pieces of the zipper tabs and stitch.

23. Flip right-side out.

24. Use wash-away tape to make up a three-layered zippy sandwich with the Lining Zipper Casing right-side up on the bottom, the zipper right-side up in the middle, and the Exterior Zipper Casing wrong-side up on the top.

25. Use a zipper foot to stitch.

26. Flip right-side out and topstitch ⅛" from the stitched line.

27. Repeat steps 24–26 to make the other side of the Zipper Casing.

28.

28. Pass the Main Body Binding and Zipper Casing Binding through a tape maker to iron the folds.

29.

29. Stitch the Zipper Casing Binding and the curved ends of the Lining Zipper Casing right sides together.

30.

30. Fold the binding to the Exterior Zipper Casing and topstitch the binding, ⅛" from the folded edge.

31.

31. Repeat steps 29–30 to make the other Zipper Casing Binding.

32. Make pockets as desired on the Lining Main Body. (Refer to the Zipper Pocket and Slip Pocket instructions, pages 5-6, 8.)

33. Fold the Lining Main Body in half lengthwise and stitch the sides.

34. Flatten the 2 bottom corners, mark 4" flat bottom lines, and stitch. Trim to a ¼" seam allowance.

32.

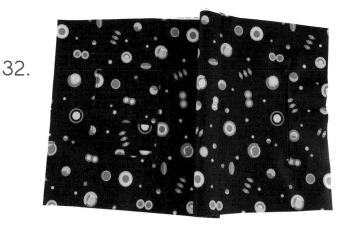

33.

34.

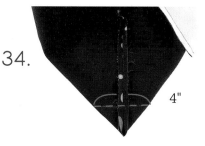

4"

35.

35. With the Lining Zipper Casing and the Lining Main Body right sides together, match the raw edges of the Zipper Casing with the top edge of the Lining Main Body.

36.

36. Baste the Zipper Casing to the Lining Main Body.

37. Fully insert the Lining Main Body wrong-side out into the Exterior Main Body right-side out. Baste the top edge. Be careful NOT to baste the curved ends of the Zipper Casing.

37.

38.

38. Stitch the Main Body Binding and the top edge of the Lining Main Body right sides together. Be careful NOT to baste the curved ends of the Zipper Casing.

39. Fold the binding to the Exterior Main Body and topstitch ⅛" from the folded edge.

39.

40.

40. Fold the curved side of the Zipper Casing down to ½" from the bottom edge of the Main Body Decorative Strip and stitch.

Materials

- One 1¼" Self-Covered Button
- Fabric A – 1 yard
- Fabric B – 1 yard

Tote Bag

Cutting and Fusing Instructions

Cutting sizes include a ⅜" seam allowance.

Fabric A

Exterior Main Body*	2 pieces 15¾" x 13¾"	Iron with heavyweight interfacing.
Exterior Gusset	2 pieces 16" x 6¼"	Iron with heavyweight interfacing.
Exterior Base	1 piece 6¼" x 13¾"	Iron with heavyweight interfacing.
Exterior Pockets	2 pieces from the Exterior Pocket pattern	See Step 3 to iron half of the pocket with heavyweight interfacing.
1¼" Self-Covered Button fabric	1 circle 2¼" in diameter	

Fabric B		
Lining Main Body*	1 piece 36¼" x 13¾"	
Lining Gusset	2 pieces 16" x 6¼"	
Handles	2 strips from the Handle pattern	Refer to the Handles pattern to iron with heavyweight interfacing.
Ties	4 strips 1½" x 12"	
Button Loop	1 strip 1½" x 10"	

*Main Body pattern is for handle, pocket, and button loop placement.

Sewing Instructions

1. Fold the handle in half lengthwise, right sides together, and stitch.

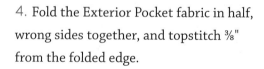

1.

2. Turn right-side out and iron the seam to the center. Topstitch ⅛" from the long edges.

2.

3.

4.

3. Iron the heavyweight interfacing on the lower half of the wrong side of the Exterior Pocket fabric.

4. Fold the Exterior Pocket fabric in half, wrong sides together, and topstitch ⅜" from the folded edge.

5. Position the Exterior Pocket at the bottom center of the Exterior Main Body according to the Main Body pattern.

5.

6.

6. Baste the sides of the Exterior Pocket.

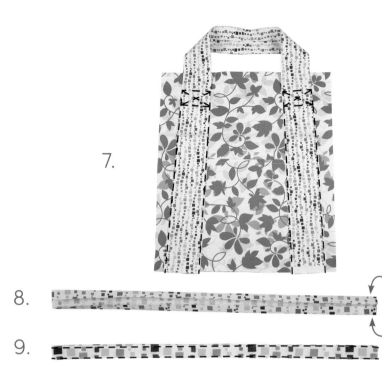

7.

7. Position the handle on top of the Exterior Main Body according to the Main Body pattern. Place the handle seam and Exterior Main Body right sides together. Topstitch the handle ⅛" from the edges.

8. Pass the Button Loop and Tie fabrics through a tape maker and iron the folds.

8.

9. Iron the Button Loop and Tie fabrics in half again. Topstitch ⅛" from the long edges.

9.

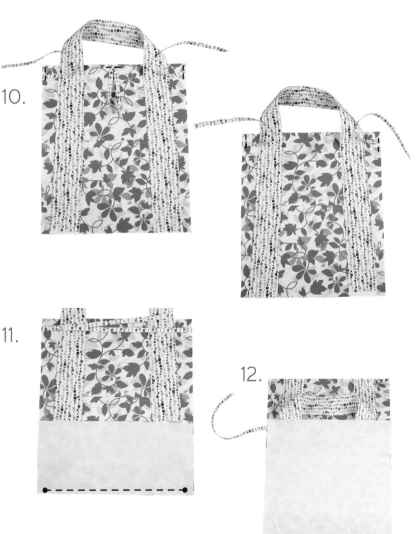

10.

10. Baste the ties at the sides, 1" from the top of the Exterior Main Bodies. Fold the Button Loop in half and baste the short raw edges at the top center edge of the Back Main Body.

11. Stitch one of the long edges of the Exterior Base and the bottom edge of the Front Main Body, right sides together, stopping ⅜" from the sides.

11.

12. Repeat on the other long edge of the Exterior Base and the bottom edge of the Back Exterior Main Body, right sides together, stopping ⅜" from the sides.

12.

13. Stitch the long edges of the Exterior Gusset and the side of the Main Body, right sides together, stopping ⅜" from the bottom edge.

14. Stitch the short edge of the Exterior Gusset and the short edge of the Exterior Base, right sides together, stopping ⅜" from the sides.

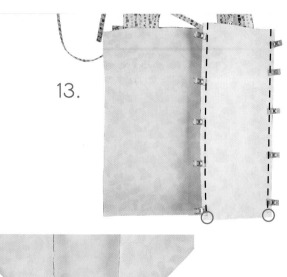

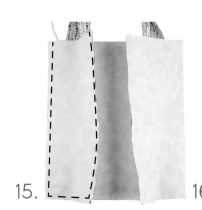

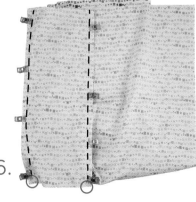

15. Repeat steps 13 & 14 to stitch the other Exterior Gusset with the Exterior Main Body and Base.

16. Stitch the long edges of the Lining Gusset and the side of the Lining Main Body, right sides together, stopping ⅜" from the bottom edge.

17. Clip the Lining Main Body at the corners and turn the fabric to align with the short edge of the bottom edge of the Gusset. Be careful NOT to clip the stitch. Stitch starting and stopping ⅜" from the sides.

18. Repeat steps 16 & 17 to stitch the other Lining Gusset with the Lining Main Body, leaving an opening at one side.

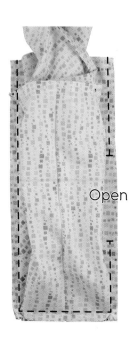

Open

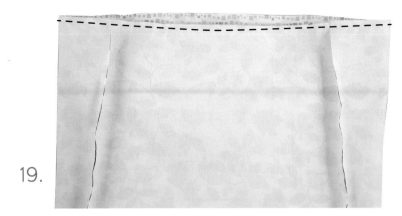

19.

19. Fully insert the Lining Main Body right-side out into the Exterior Main Body wrong-side out. Stitch the top edge.

20. Turn right-side out through the opening. Topstitch, ¼" from the top edge.

21. Fold the long edges of the handles to the center line. Stitch as shown.

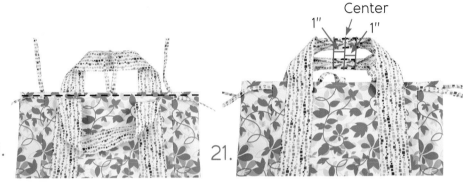

20.   **21.**

22. Follow the instructions to make a Self-Covered Button (page 9).

23. Sew the button to the Exterior Main Body.

22.

23.

Resources

Ranger Inkssentials Wonder Tape
double-sided, heat-resistant
clear Mylar tape

U-Handbag
(u-handbag.com)
bag bottom stiffener

*Ask at your local quilt shop for fabrics
by these manufacturers.*

Free Spirit
(http://freespiritfabric.com)

  Foldable Eco Bag

  Cutie Backpack

  Tote Bag (yellow)

  Four-Piece Eco Bag

Art Gallery Fabrics
(www.artgalleryquilts.com)

  Moon Bag

  Fresh Shoulder Bag

  Three-Layer Handbag

Anthology Fabrics
(www.anthologyfabrics.com)

  Citrus Handbag

  Tote Bag (blue)

Benartex, Inc.
(www.benartex.com)

  Spicy Girl Messenger Bag

Andover Fabrics™
(www.andoverfabrics.com)
Expandable Zipper Tote Bag

About Moya's Workshop

Moya's Workshop, located in the heart of central Taipei, specializes in importing quilting and patchwork supplies from the United States and Europe to Taiwan. The team behind Moya's Workshop includes a group of talented professionals drawn from the fields of design, art, and photography. Current areas of interest range from bag design and independent publishing to professional designer development and management.

Julia Chen earned a degree in Sewing and Fashion Design. She has over 30 years of design and teaching experience and is the main designer of the purses and bags in this book. Julia lives with her family in Taipei, Taiwan.

Nana Wu is the editor as well as a creative force in her own right at Moya's Workshop. She has over six years of machine sewing and quilting experience and also designs sewing projects. Nana lives and works in Taichung, Taiwan.

Moya Hu, the owner of Moya's Workshop, hosts a popular handmade-themed blog that has had more than 2 million visitors since its inception. She started quilting in 2006 and has already authored two successful books on handmade topics published in the local market. Moya works as a finance controller in the daytime and views crafting as a passionate hobby that helps to relieve pressure. She lives with her cute dog, Bogi, in Taipei, Taiwan.

Visit Moya's Workshop blog:
http://tw.myblog.yahoo.com/moya-hu/

More AQS Books

This is only a small selection of the books available from the American Quilter's Society. AQS books are known worldwide for timely topics, clear writing, beautiful color photos, and accurate illustrations and patterns. The following books are available from your local bookseller, quilt shop, or public library.

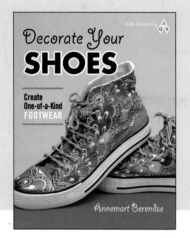

#8766

#8354

#8532

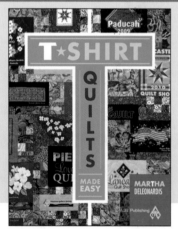

#8664

#8762

#8671

#8663

#8763

#8768